TRAIN YOUR BRAIN

How Your Brain Learns Best

BY JEFF SZPIRGLAS AND DANIELLE SAINT-ONGE

CRABTREE
PUBLISHING COMPANY
WWW.CRABTREEBOOKS.COM

Authors: Jeff Szpirglas, Danielle Saint-Onge

Series Research and Development: Reagan Miller

Editors: Janine Deschenes, Kenneth Lane

Proofreader: Wendy Scavuzzo

Design: Margaret Amy Salter

Photo research: Margaret Amy Salter

Production coordinator and
  Prepress technician: Margaret Amy Salter, Abigail Smith

Print coordinator: Katherine Berti

Consultant: Kenneth Lane, Bioscientist and Science Writer and Editor

Acknowledgement: Eleanor A. Maguire FMedSci, FRS,
  University College London
  Barbara Arrowsmith-Young, Arrowsmith School

Photo Credits

Shutterstock: ©StockStudio p 12

Wikimedia: Taeyebar p 13 (br)

All other images from Shutterstock

Library and Archives Canada Cataloguing in Publication

Szpirglas, Jeff, author
    Train your brain : how your brain learns best / Jeff Szpirglas,
Danielle Saint-Onge.

(Exploring the brain)
Includes bibliographical references and index.
Issued in print and electronic formats.
ISBN 978-0-7787-3498-7 (hardcover).--
ISBN 978-0-7787-3510-6 (softcover).--
ISBN 978-1-4271-1933-9 (HTML)

    1. Learning--Physiological aspects--Juvenile literature. 2. Brain--
Physiology--Juvenile literature. 3. Learning strategies--Juvenile
literature. I. Saint-Onge, Danielle, author II. Title.

QP408.S98 2017   j612.8'2   C2017-906547-5
                                          C2017-906548-3

Library of Congress Cataloging-in-Publication Data

Names: Szpirglas, Jeff, author. | Saint-Onge, Danielle, 1982- author.
Title: Train your brain : how your brain learns best / Jeff Szpirglas and
    Danielle Saint-Onge.
Description: New York, New York : Crabtree Publishing Company,
    [2018] | Series: Exploring the brain | Includes bibliographical
    references and index.
Identifiers: LCCN 2017059665 (print) | LCCN 2017060341 (ebook) |
    ISBN 9781427119339 (Electronic HTML) |
    ISBN 9780778734987 (reinforced library binding) |
    ISBN 9780778735106 (pbk.)
Subjects: LCSH: Neuroplasticity--Juvenile literature. | Neural circuitry-
    -Juvenile literature. | Brain--Growth--Juvenile literature. | Memory--
    Physiological aspects--Juvenile literature.
Classification: LCC QP361.5 (ebook) | LCC QP361.5 .S97 2018 (print) |
    DDC 612.8/2--dc23
LC record available at https://lccn.loc.gov/2017059665

Crabtree Publishing Company

www.crabtreebooks.com   1-800-387-7650

Printed in the U.S.A./022018/CG20171220

Published in Canada
Crabtree Publishing
616 Welland Ave.
St. Catharines, Ontario
L2M 5V6

Published in the United States
Crabtree Publishing
PMB 59051
350 Fifth Avenue, 59th Floor
New York, New York 10118

Published in the United Kingdom
Crabtree Publishing
Maritime House
Basin Road North, Hove
BN41 1WR

Published in Australia
Crabtree Publishing
3 Charles Street
Coburg North
VIC, 3058

Table of Contents

CHAPTER 1

How Your BRAIN WORKS

Have you ever wondered why you have trouble remembering things when you feel scared or sleepy? Do you notice times when your mind feels clearer, and you are able to focus? There are specific reasons why we feel these ways. We process certain types of information in different ways, depending on the situations in which we find ourselves. It all comes back to our body's most incredible organ: the brain.

This book is designed to teach you about how your brain works, and to give you tips, tools, and strategies that will allow you to better harness your mind and learning potential, both in and out of school.

Your brain has an amazing ability to make changes and reorganize itself throughout your lifetime. It creates connections which allow you to develop new skills and respond well to different environments. The goal is to encourage you to make conscious and proactive decisions so you can be the most incredible you possible.

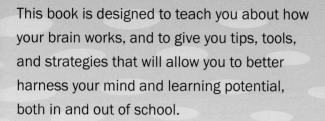

You can improve your skills and learning abilities by training your brain. Read on to find out more.

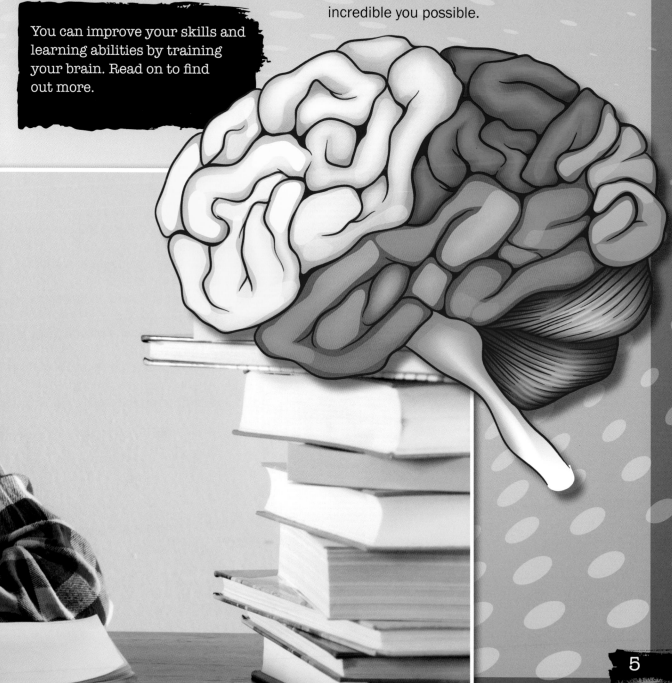

Take your hands and make fists. Then, put your fists together. You're looking at a pretty good representation of your brain, in terms of its size, as well as the two hemispheres. But if you look deep within the structure of the brain, you'll find tiny little nerve cells, called neurons. These are what make learning possible.

Neurons

Neurons are made up of three main parts: the **cell body**; the **axon**, which sends signals to other nerve cells; and the branch-like **dendrites**, which receive messages from other neurons. For a better idea of what neurons look like, turn to page 42.

Your brain has somewhere between 86 and 100 billion neurons. That's a lot! Each one of those neurons has the ability to form connections, called synapses, with other neurons. These synapses are important, because your brain is using them to make connections using the knowledge and experience you accumulate every single day.

Synapses

The connections between the neurons in your body are known as synapses. These are important, because when you learn about something—and actually work hard to understand and comprehend it—your brain forms new synaptic connections. But what are synapses, exactly? They're actually tiny gaps between neighboring neurons. Electrical signals are fired across the synapses from one neuron to another.

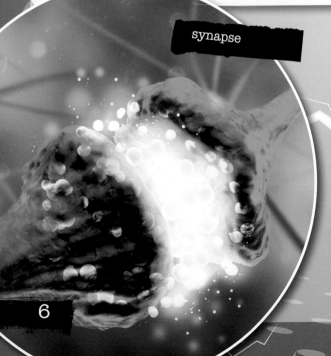

synapse

You've got even more synapses than you do neurons—anywhere from 100 trillion to 1,000 trillion! All of these connections enable parts of your brain to communicate with other parts of your body, allowing you to learn and remember. Learning is happening all the time. It might be when you read this book, when you're playing the drums, building a model, or even having a conversation on the phone with a friend.

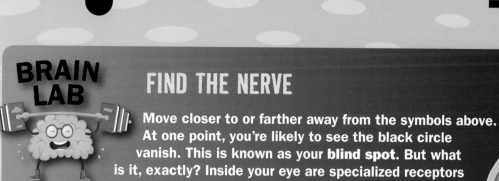

FIND THE NERVE

Move closer to or farther away from the symbols above. At one point, you're likely to see the black circle vanish. This is known as your **blind spot**. But what is it, exactly? Inside your eye are specialized receptors that sense light. Your eye is full of them, except in one spot—that's the **optic nerve**, which is where the information goes from your eye to your brain (and back again). When you see that spot disappear, it's because you've hit the blind spot taken up by your optic nerve.

blind spot

Take Care of Your Neurons!

Your body is great at healing itself. If you cut your finger, your body will repair the broken blood vessels and seal the cut, sometimes with a scar. But if you damage an area of your brain, you won't regrow old neurons. At least, not to repair that damaged area. But, your brain can make new neurons in some parts, such as in your **hippocampus** (the area for learning and memory). This is known as **neurogenesis**.

Exercising Your Brain into Shape?

There is evidence that aerobic exercise (such as running, or jumping jacks—if you're up to it right now) might actually help with neurogenesis... at least, in some of our furry friends. In a study published in 2016, researchers at the University of Jyväskylä in Finland studied rats that were put on running regimens for 6 to 8 weeks. What they found was that rats that were good at running long distances were also the ones with the most new hippocampal neurons. The rats that tended to get on the running wheel got 2 to 3 times more new neurons than the rats that didn't. This was similar to earlier studies in mice.

Some scientists estimate there might be 250,000 neurons produced each minute during the time of peak human development in the womb.

Hanging out in the Hippocampus

If the neurons and synaptic connections in your brain are the connections that help you to learn, then in what part of your brain does learning take place? Around 75%, or three-quarters, of all of your neural connections are in your brain's cerebrum. This large section of your brain includes the outer layer and many of the inner parts of your brain, such as the hippocampus.

But if you're looking to boost your learning and memory, the other structure to explore is the hippocampus. This is the structure involved with neurogenesis. The larger the hippocampus, the better people tend to be at remembering things. As you get older, it's the first part of the brain that gets smaller—but it can also grow and form connections, even into adulthood.

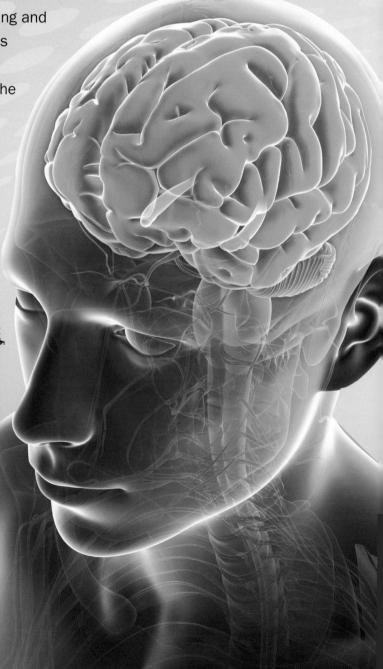

The hippocampus is made up of two small, seahorse-shaped structures.

8

BRAIN LAB

MEMORY GAME

Want to work on boosting your mind and form new neural connections? Try some memory games every day. As you'll see from examples coming up (such as the amazing development of the hippocampi of London cab drivers), memorization exercises are linked to increased **matter** in the hippocampus.

Look at this list of words for around 10 seconds, then look away and try to remember the words.

HAT BIT PIN COT BET

Now check out this list for around 20 seconds:

NUT SAP LOB NIT RAD TOP MAP LIP INK MAT

Use It or Lose It

When your neurons aren't firing and maintaining their connections, these connections can start to shrink away. This type of shrinking is known as disuse atrophy. But the good news is that you have it in you to maintain those connections, and even form new ones. Turn the page to find out more!

Hippocampus and Exercise

Can exercise alone make a hippocampus grow? In 2009, a researcher at the University of Pittsburgh decided to put it to the test. The study involved 120 adults from 60 to 80 years old who were still mentally sound, but not physically fit.

These participants were put into groups of those who stretched and those who walked three times a week for 40 minutes. When the study concluded a year later, MRI imaging revealed that the hippocampus in the group that had been walking instead of stretching had grown by around 2%. That may not seem like much, but when aging, the hippocampus tends to shrink by around half a percent each year!

CHAPTER 2

NEUROPLASTICITY

For many years, scientists thought that the brain was an organ that couldn't change. Older research on the brain suggested that people were born with sets of strengths and weaknesses that could last a lifetime. But new research is showing that brains can change throughout our lives. With some training, they are able to grow stronger and more resilient.

Your brain can grow stronger, not unlike your muscles, which can grow and change with more vigorous use and care.

THINK ABOUT IT!

Using the information about neurons in this book, explain how your brain is able to learn. What is neuroplasticity? Describe in your own words.

What is Neuroplasticity?

Neuroplasticity is a change in your nervous system. This could mean a change in how your brain works or functions, or even the way it is structured. The neurons that make up the pathways and connections in your brain are flexible. This means that they can break and remake connections with other neurons. When they do this, they stretch and shift like a piece of rubbery plastic.

Yes, your brain can literally change, or physically remodel itself. As you read on, you'll learn about studies that show new connections can form between the neurons of your brain—and areas of the brain can even grow denser with these new neural pathways. To grow denser means that there is more matter in the brain.

How Does It Work?

As you learn new skills or memorize new information, your brain gets a bit of a workout, just like you can improve your **cardiovascular** fitness by training on a treadmill, or slowly increasing how far you go jogging.

One great way to create new connections in your brain is to learn a new skill, such as playing a musical instrument.

Neuroplasticity in the Real World

A growing body of research and case studies have found that people of all ages have shown signs of neuroplasticity when their brains are put to the test and they are trying hard. And that's just it—in both of the case studies described below, the people involved weren't just sitting around and wishing their brains would develop. To train their brains, they had to focus and study. The results are staggering.

CASE STUDY 1:
LONDON CAB DRIVERS

London, England, has around 26,000 criss-crossing streets in a small area that cab drivers need to know. Cab drivers can spend three or four years navigating these streets, studying maps and landmarks to get "The Knowledge" of London's layout. This includes taking a set of tough exams that can eliminate around half of the applicants. Only those with passing marks can move on to drive London's famous black taxicabs.

In a now-famous study published in 2000, researchers followed a group of London cab-driver trainees for four years. By the time they finished the rigorous training period, those who passed their exams had greater **gray matter** volume in part of the hippocampus compared to when they began their training.

The conclusion? The hippocampus helps process the **visual-spatial information** that taxi drivers need to know when navigating the thousands of streets and landmarks. All of that time spent learning London's layout may have increased the neuronal connections in the hippocampus, or encouraged new neurons to grow. This is because the hippocampus is one of the few brain regions where new neurons are born.

CASE STUDY 2:
THE WOMAN WHO CHANGED HER BRAIN

As a child, Barbara Arrowsmith-Young was **diagnosed** with what we would today call a learning disability. She had trouble processing language concepts. Until she was in her 20s, she did not understand the content of much of what she read or heard. She wrote and read backwards, and often got lost when she was reading or listening to others speak.

In her late 20s, frustrated at the challenges she was facing, Barbara came up with a plan. To help train her brain, she started to draw clock faces. Carefully drawing the hour and minute hand, she would spend hours studying her drawings to focus on the relationship between the hands of the clock. Eventually, her hard work paid off—forcing the neurons in her brain to fire in new ways. The new neural pathways that developed in her brain helped her overcome her disability with understanding concepts. She began to apply these techniques in other areas. In 1980, Arrowsmith-Young started a school in Toronto to teach students her own specialized techniques to improve brain function. The school currently identifies 19 areas of thinking and learning, and has built a program to help improve the functioning of these areas.

Barbara Arrowsmith-Young's program has been used in 90 educational organizations in Canada, the United States, Australia, New Zealand, and some countries in Asia.

CHAPTER 3

GROWTH MINDSET

Stanford University psychologist Carol Dweck spent years studying what motivates people. She noticed that the way people view themselves affects their ability to do something. She studied how people fit onto a scale of how they view themselves—from believing they have fixed abilities ("I'm not good at math"), to embracing the growth of their abilities ("This math is hard, but I will keep trying and learn from my mistakes"). The latter view is what Dweck calls a **growth mindset**. Her work on fixed and growth mindsets is now being used to businesses and schools in many countries to help workers and students learn new skills.

What is a Growth Mindset?

Do you think a course is too hard? That you just might not be cut out for something, whether it's acing a math test, or being able to make the football team? These are all traits of what Dweck has called a **fixed mindset**. This is a belief that your talents and abilities were fixed, or predetermined, when you were born. This kind of thinking often gets people to doubt their abilities. They might not try something because they don't think they can do it. This means that they do not take the risks and make the mistakes that allow their brains to learn and grow new neural pathways.

If you have a fixed mindset, you might give up when you think you've reached your limit, instead of pushing yourself forward and allowing your brain to make new connections. Similarly, those people who have the belief that they are smart, and that what they're doing is always perfect, might face the same problem— this fixed type of thinking doesn't open the brain to learning new ways of seeing things or overcoming challenges.

Having a growth mindset, on the other hand, is the belief that your abilities can be shaped and developed as you persevere with a task. If you have a growth mindset, you might try something new, even if you aren't sure if you'll succeed. You don't give up when you encounter a problem and you try to see a problem or situation from different perspectives to succeed. Having this mindset puts you in the frame of mind that, when you're learning something new, you'll get better as you stick to things. This mindset also helps us learn that setbacks and mistakes are things you can use as learning opportunities.

Beware the "False" Growth Mindset

To have a growth mindset, you can't just say it—you have to live it. And not everybody can have a growth mindset in all areas all the time. Even now, as you read this, you might have fixed views about some things, and a growth mindset about others. Watch for the triggers that get you thinking you might not be able to achieve a goal. Dweck herself even talks about how people with growth mindsets have some fixed-mindset triggers. Do you know what yours are?

Growth Mindset in the Classroom

There's a classic story book about a little train that nobody believed could carry its heavy load on a long journey. But with perseverance and the growth-mindset mantra "I think I can, I think I can," the train succeeded. We learn these key concepts at school with our teachers, and that's why there is so much research being done on how growth mindsets are taught in classrooms.

Research being done on classrooms that have actively taught and employed a growth-mindset perspective show students with higher achievement on standardized tests. But they also have better marks on report cards and higher self-esteem overall. When we read stories like *The Little Engine that Could*, we are learning how others have applied a growth mindset, and helping to apply it to our own daily lives. Certain subjects at school can seem daunting. So it's important that your school practices and teaches you how to use a growth mindset so you feel prepared to conquer whatever comes your way.

I THINK I CAN! I THINK I CAN! I THINK I CAN!

Growth Mindset Helps All Students

In a study published in 2016, researchers looked at data for around 168,000 Chilean students in grade 10 preparing for their national achievement test in language and math. Students were first posed questions in a survey that explored whether they had a growth mindset. Those students identified with a growth mindset were much more likely to score in the top 20% of the test, while those with more fixed views were much more likely to score in the lower 20%. What's just as notable is that those with a growth mindset did better on the test than their fixed-mindset peers, whether they were from a low- or high-income neighborhood.

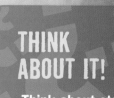

THINK ABOUT IT!

Think about strategies that work for you at school to help you overcome challenges or do well on tests or assignments. Do you use a growth mindset? How could you change some of your strategies so they fit better with a growth mindset?

Do You Have a Mathematical Mindset?

Jo Boaler, a math professor at Stanford University, has built on Dwick's growth mindset theory specifically to help students in the math classroom. Her key belief is that people are not born with brains hardwired for math. She thinks that, with hard work and a growth mindset, everyone can learn math to the highest levels. Like Dwick, her work has focused on shifting the thinking of teachers and students to using growth mindsets, and this involves setting up several math class norms, as shown below.

How many of these math class "norms" do you see at your school?

1. Everyone Can Learn Math to the Highest Levels
The belief that only some people are good at math is a false one. You too can understand math concepts with belief and perseverance.

2. Mistakes Are Valuable
The best learning happens from mistakes, which help your brain to grow.

3. Questions Are Very Important
Questions are what show your thinking and push you to stretch your understanding.

4. Math Is About Creativity and Making Sense
Math is about finding the patterns in nature.

5. Math Is About Connections and Communicating
The memorization of number facts doesn't show your understanding, or depth. Math is about seeing patterns and understanding them, especially through talk with others.

6. Depth Is More Important Than Speed
Math isn't about being the fastest. To think deeply, it's important to take your time and understand what you're learning about.

7. Math Is About Learning, Not Performing
It takes time to learn new concepts.

Growth Mindset Quiz

Can you identify which of these statements is a fixed versus a growth mindset? Being able to identify the differences will help you to better shape your point of view over things that happen to you in your daily life. The better you are at shifting your point of view to a growth mindset, the more successful you will be in tackling challenges both at home and at school.

1. The harder you work at something, the better you will be at it.
2. Only a few people will be truly good at sports; you have to be born with the ability.
3. Very smart people do not need to try hard.
4. I like my work best when I can do it perfectly without any mistakes.
5. An important reason why I do my school work is that I enjoy learning new things.

Answers: 1. Growth 2. Fixed 3. Fixed 4. Fixed 5. Growth

The Brain and Executive Functioning

Imagine a very busy airport with planes flying in at different times to different locations, and different passengers with different needs. A successful airport needs a team of air traffic controllers who guide the planes and passengers to the right areas to keep accidents and delays from happening. That's a good analogy of your brain's **executive functions**, which pilot you through your day. Your executive functioning is controlled by your brain's prefrontal cortex (below). This part of your brain develops more slowly than your **amygdala**, which can cause you to experience challenges to your executive functioning ability.

Amygdala

When you're scared or stressed, your amygdala is activated, putting you in fight-or-flight mode. Your ability to use your executive functioning is impaired, because information stays in the amygdala, and isn't going to your prefrontal cortex. This explains why it's hard to remember things when you're scared or stressed, as no information is being sent to the hippocampus for long-term storage.

Prefrontal Cortex (PFC)

This is the part of your brain responsible for your executive functioning skills. The strategies that you will be reading about throughout the book involve consciously activating your PFC, so that you can do your best learning and focusing. Your brain actually grows and develops from back to front, which means that your PFC is the last section of your brain to develop and reach maturity.

Executive functioning involves five key skills that all of us need to get through our day. These are regulated by the prefrontal cortex of our brains, which doesn't reach maturity until your early 20s. So if these skills seem tricky to master, they just might be!

Working Memory

Can you remember and retrieve memories to complete a task, which might be academic, such as math facts, or might also be social, such as people's names and background information?

Social Communication

This is the ability to have a successful conversation with someone by recognizing the verbal and nonverbal cues they may give you. These cues can include body language, tone of voice, and eye contact.

Organization

Keeping track of your binders, knowing where your papers and things are throughout the day. Does your desk or locker look as though a tornado blew through it? But also, how do you organize your time to complete tasks? Do you get stuck on one test question and can't move on? Or are you always finishing assignments at the very last minute right before they're due, or asking for an extension?

Adaptability

Can you be flexible when things change? Does this make you upset, or can you handle changes as they happen? Do you go with the flow? For example, what if your hockey game is cancelled, and you've been looking forward to it all week. How do you react?

Impulse Control

Can you hold in a negative thought or behavior without feeling the need to express it? For instance, shouting out during a lesson? Or when you blurt out the first thing that comes to your mind when someone asks you a question?

Executive Functioning and You

Are you finding it harder to manage in some of the areas you just learned about? That is totally normal. In adolescence, your prefrontal cortex goes through a big change. This can affect your ability to use executive functioning skills. You might be more likely to show impulsive behavior—such as choosing to go out with your friends instead of finishing this book; or have trouble planning, such as leaving your homework to the very last second. Because the parts of your brain that control your working memory and organizational skills are still developing, it's even harder to manage all that homework, your soccer practice, chores, and other responsibilities.

Brain scientists used to think that the majority of brain development and neuron pruning happened in babies and ended by around age five. However, Jay Giedd and a team of researchers at McGill University in Montreal began to take MRIs of kids every two years to chart the way the brain changed during adolescence. They noted many significant changes in the prefrontal cortex of the brain throughout adolescence, which would explain the difficulties that you and other teens may face in **self-regulating** and using their executive-functioning skills.

We use the term "pruning" because brain-cell connections are removed in the brain just as extra branches and leaves on trees are pruned.

So what changes did they notice? Not only did the prefrontal cortex continue to grow in size, they discovered that from ages 13 to 18 this area continued to have neurons and their synapses grow and expand. Most surprisingly though, they saw many connections between brain cells lost. The process of losing connections between brain cells is called pruning. When this pruning is complete, the brain grows white matter (myelin) around the connections to strengthen the speed at which they carry messages and communicate. So the more you use and build your neural connections, the more those connections will stay and develop. The less you use them, the more get pruned away. It's what they call the "use it or lose it" principle.

Self-regulating refers to being able to control your actions, thoughts, and emotions so that they are in your best interests. Examples of self-regulation include limiting how much pizza you should eat, or controlling your emotional reaction to something so that you don't lash out at others.

Use It or Lose It!

How is your prefrontal cortex doing? The chart below is a mini test of how well your brain is using its "tool box" of executive functioning skills. Read the statements in the "Question" column of the chart below and check "Always" "Sometimes" or "Never." In which areas are you doing well? Which do you need to focus on and practice?

Question	Always	Sometimes	Never
I get upset and angry when even minor things go unplanned.			
I have difficulty finishing my sentences and/or thoughts.			
I get in trouble for shouting things out in class and talking out of turn.			
I forget to bring home and hand in homework.			
I have trouble using my time to finish my homework.			
I have trouble when working with detailed instructions.			
I get stuck trying to find solutions to problems.			
My workspace (desk, locker) is messy.			

The more we recognize and practice these skills, and put tools in place to help us be successful, the more connections we are actually building in our brain.

When you use your executive-functioning skills, you are increasing the connections between neurons in your brain and therefore making those skills stronger. There are a range of strategies out there that you can use to "work out" your brain and increase those connections. Try some of these strategies that strengthen your executive-functioning skills.

So, What's in Your Toolbox?

A great way to think about it is a toolbelt of skills that you have to get through your day. The better your box is organized and the more tools you have, the better you are able to function over the course of your day.

Study Survival Guide

- Have you ever tried recording your voice reading your study notes using your iPod or phone? Sometimes saying the information out loud and listening to yourself helps to activate and store it in your long-term memory.
- When studying for a test, try writing different sections in different colors. This can help your brain better store the information because you can visualize it clearly in your head as you are studying.

Map It Out!

You know that agenda that's sitting untouched at the bottom of your bag? Use it. The better you can map out step by step what needs to be done and when, the more successful you will be at completing tasks. Write important dates down yourself. Don't rely on social media or your phone to tell you when things are due.

Time It!

Do you have a timer on your electronic device? Try setting it for 15-minute study session chunks. Then take a five-minute brain break where you can walk or move around. This helps your brain to stay focused on the task and to better store the information you need for the task in your memory.

CHAPTER 4

MINDFULNESS

Why Stress Sucks!

When you're continually stressed or worrying, you risk triggering your fight-or-flight response. The fight-or-flight response is your body's reaction to something threatening. This response is caused by your **sympathetic nervous system**, which acts similar to the gas pedal in the car. When stressed, parts of your brain send messages to your adrenal glands to send **adrenaline** into your bloodstream. It increases your heartbeat, and pumps blood to your muscles to get you ready to move away. Sure, it's helpful if you need to run away from a threat—but too much of this response is not good for the body or the brain.

But how can you find ways to train your brain to de-stress? That's the work of your **parasympathetic nervous system**. Some experts suggest being more mindful.

26

Read This... Then Relax

Once you're finished reading this paragraph, make sure you're in a comfortable seated position, in a quiet space, and close your eyes. Take a moment to notice what's going on around you. Notice the way your body is positioned and the way you are breathing in and out. Focus on that breathing. Are you ready? Close your eyes and try it.

What is Mindfulness?

Did you take a few moments to try that? Thanks for being mindful. Your body and your brain will probably thank you, too. Mindfulness is a way of taking control of your attention and focusing it on the present moment. When you are practicing mindfulness, you are not worrying about things you've done, or things that might happen to you in the future, such as whether you'll bomb an upcoming assignment. By focusing on the "here and now," the brain can stop stressing about the "what ifs." Mindfulness is achieved through quiet **meditation**. This is a mental exercise in which you block out external noises, distractions, and, of course, your own running thoughts.

There is evidence that reducing stress using mindfulness can help lessen the mental and physical symptoms of pain, **depression**, and **anxiety** (and sometimes even prevent them) in both adults and children. Even big companies such as Google have been known to set up mindful meditation sessions and classes for their employees, to help them focus and be more productive workers.

BRAIN LAB

Are You Mindful?

One of the most important steps in mindfulness is reflecting on our thoughts and behaviors to change our perspective, but also to activate different brain pathways. The more we can calm our bodies down, the more we can access and use our prefrontal cortex to help us make mindful decisions versus instinctual and fear-based ones. So as a first step, see if you can figure out which behaviors represent mindful pathways.

1. I forget a person's name almost as soon as I've been told it for the first time.
2. After I read a passage, I am able to summarize what I have just read.
3. After my friend shares a story with me, I am able to respond to what he/she has said
4. I do not notice changes inside my body, such as my heart beating faster or my muscles getting tense.
5. I do jobs or tasks automatically, without being aware of what I'm doing.

Answers: 1. Not mindful 2. Mindful 3. Mindful 4. Not mindful 5. Not mindful

Your Brain on Mindfulness

In 2007, Norman Farb, a neurologist at the University of Toronto, noticed that we use two sets of neural networks, or networks made up of neurons, to interact with the world around us.

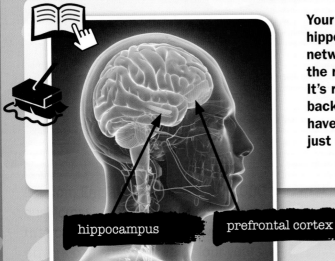

hippocampus   prefrontal cortex

Your default neural network includes the hippocampus and prefrontal cortex. This is the network that's used for planning, as well as all the random, daydreamy thoughts you might have. It's running even when you're chilling out in your backyard, then begin thinking about things you have to get done (homework! chores!) instead of just taking a moment to relax.

Your direct experience neural network uses parts of your brain such as the insula and the anterior cingulate cortex. These parts are important in shifting your attention. When you're in this mode, you're focusing more on what's happening to you in the present, such as what smells are in the air or what sounds are in your environment. This network allows you to notice these things without worrying or thinking about what they mean.

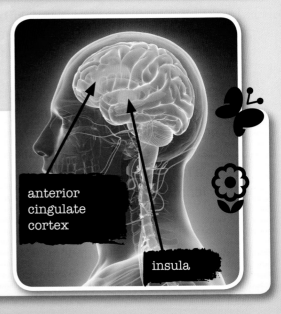

anterior cingulate cortex

insula

When you're in default mode, you tend to focus less on the senses that are heightened in the direct experience network. Similarly, when you're in direct experience mode, you're less focused on day-to-day worries and stresses.

This might explain why taking the time to slowly savor your food and notice the flavors makes it taste that much better. Other studies have shown that people who practice mindfulness may be more aware of their own unconscious thinking and processes, and have more cognitive control.

Mindfulness in the Classroom

Studies have shown that mindfulness-based approaches can help reduce stresses and even improve academic success. In one study that lasted for three years, teachers at a middle school in south central Los Angeles were trained to teach relaxation skills to their students in sessions lasting five weeks. These included discussions on how the body reacted to stress, as well as mindfulness meditations that involved breathing exercises. Overall, the researchers found that GPA scores of students given the mindfulness training increased (from 10 to 20%) versus those who did not. However, students needed to take at least two mindfulness courses in order to see their GPA scores improve.

When we relax using strategies such as meditation, our bodies and brains respond in something called the **relaxation response.** This causes the brain to release chemicals that reduce stress and can increase blood flow to the brain. The more blood flow the brain receives, the better it works.

THINK ABOUT IT!

What is the direct experience network and how does it relate to mindfulness? Can you think of one way you can use your direct experience network to practice mindfulness?

Meditation and Mindfulness

Meditation is one way to practice mindfulness—and a successful one. It is a series of techniques that focus on relaxing the body, but also on providing a sense of well-being. Often, this involves sitting in a calm, quiet area and focusing your attention on something specific, such as the rhythm of your breathing. The goal is to minimize distractions and calm the mind.

Recent studies have suggested that meditation might have an impact on the actual structure of your brain, particularly as you age. By your late 20s, your brain's volume and weight slowly begins to drop. A 2015 study by UCLA researchers compared the brains of 50 people who mediated for at least four years, and around 20 years on average, with 50 people who did not meditate. The study revealed that the meditators lost less gray matter as they aged than the non-meditators. Meanwhile, a 2011 study noticed that 20 participants in a course on mindfulness-based stress reduction had increased thickness in the hippocampus area of the brain (associated with emotion regulation), and a decrease in volume in the amygdala, which is associated with responses for fear and anxiety.

Buddhists from Tibet, a region in the Himalayan mountains, are well known for their practice and experience in meditation. Some monks put more than 10,000 hours of work and practice into it. This hard work, focusing on compassion and happiness, can also change the way your brain works.

Psychology professor Richard Davidson has spent years analyzing images of the brain activity of experienced meditators. In some tests, the act of meditation stimulated areas of the brain associated with feelings of calmness. In another study, meditators were asked to shift between **states of meditation**. One state was neutral, and the other state focused on love and compassion. When Davidson analyzed the data, he noticed that the meditative states revealed that the **anterior insula region** of the brain became activated—a place associated with well-being in the rest of the body.

In another study, volunteers who did not regularly practice meditation were taught to meditate as part of an intervention program called Mindfulness-Based Stress Reduction. The study found changes in the brain associated with positive emotions, and discovered that the program had positive effects on the participants' immune system responses.

BRAIN LAB

BELLY BREATHING

Did you know that we are born able to properly breathe, but that as we age and become less in tune to our bodies, we forget how? Research shows that conscious, mindful, deep-belly breathing not only relaxes our bodies, but frees our minds, and helps our brains better take in and process information. Give this a try:

1. Sit comfortably on a pillow or on the floor with legs folded. To begin, you might find it useful to wear a tight-fitting shirt that allows you to better see your stomach and rib cage area. This will allow you to better take in your own body cues.

2. Breathe in through your nose, expanding your belly outward as you breathe. It should look as though you have swallowed a large balloon. Feel the roundness and warmth of the deep breath. Allow your ribs to slightly flare out to the sides, while the shoulders, upper chest, and abdomen remain motionless.

3. Breathe out through your nose and mouth. Feel the "balloon" of your stomach deflate and pull in, almost as if your belly button is pulling in toward your body.

4. Allow breath to flow continuously, with no pause allowed between the breaths, either between inhalation and exhalation, or between exhalation and inhalation.

CHAPTER 5

Creating CONNECTIONS

Do you like learning a new language? Perhaps French or Spanish was taught at your school. Maybe you're learning how to speak the native language of your parents, or grandparents in after-school classes, or at home with them. Regardless of what language you're learning, it's a good idea to keep practicing. Speaking two languages, called bilingualism, allows you to talk to more diverse groups of people and opens up interesting career opportunities later in life. But science is also showing that it could actually change the structure of your brain.

Two Tongues Are Brainier Than One

In a 2004 study, the brains of bilingual Europeans were compared to monolinguals (those who spoke one language). The study showed that speaking more than one language was associated with denser gray matter in the **left inferior parietal lobe**. This part of the brain is heavily associated with language. Age was also related to the study. The participants who learned a second language before they were 5 years old had greater brain volume than those who learned later. Other studies have showed that learning another language may be connected to brain changes such as cortical thickness (the thickness of the layers of the **cortex**). Learning a language later in life can alter brain structure, too. For example, some studies with people such as interpreters taking three-month language courses showed more differences in their brains than those who did not undergo any training.

left inferior parietal lobe

Rehearse Your Languages, Don't Reverse Them!

Just because you've learned a language doesn't mean you'll necessarily keep that denser gray matter in your cortex. In one study, Japanese participants took a six-week English-language course. They showed a greater gray matter density than those who didn't take the course. But a year later, the participants who kept speaking English showed more increases in gray matter than those who didn't. Those participants who stopped speaking English ended up with their gray-matter density diminishing back to the levels observed before the study started.

Age Isn't an Issue!

In a 2014 study at Penn State University, researchers observed 39 English-speaking participants learning some Chinese words. The greater the connections in their brains, the easier it was for participants to learn a new language. Although some studies have suggested it might be easier to learn languages at a younger age, the researchers were seeing changes in brain structure even in the elderly— suggesting that neuroplasticity from learning a new language can happen at any age.

Exercise and the Brain

Exercise is a powerful tool in helping your brain concentrate on mental tasks and problem-solving. In fact, research is so strong in this area, it's amazing that more schools don't make kids swap out their chairs and desks for stationary bicycles. Studies on the human brain and exercise show how active the prefrontal cortex—that super-important control center for your executive functioning—becomes during exercise. Cardiovascular activity, such as walking, cycling, and running, increases blood flow to the brain, which increases brain activity. Check out the cool ways that countries around the world are embracing this trend.

Forest Bathing:

Also called Shinrin Yoku, forest bathing became a part of the Japanese national health program in 1982. Research has proven that walking, meditating, and spending time in forests significantly reduces stress **hormones**, **blood pressure**, and **insulin** levels. All of these reductions help the body stay healthy. The trick is to walk slowly and mindfully, listening to the sounds, taking in the smells, and observing the plants and living things around you. It offers us an opportunity to unplug from our technology. So why not give your brain a break (and a boost!) and hit up a local park with some trees for some good old-fashioned nature time?

Take a Three-Day Hike

It might sound simple, but clinical studies show that taking time to unwind in nature benefits the brain. One scientist has coined the "Three-Day Effect" to explain the power spending time outdoors has on our brains. In one study, after spending three days out backpacking in nature, participants did 50% better on some creative problem-solving activities. The three days refers to the average amount of time it takes for our senses to "**recalibrate**" and pick up on things, such as smells and sounds, we might not have noticed amid the buzz of our busy, distracted lives.

Equine Therapy and Anxiety

For many people, anxiety can become so crippling that it can stop them from doing the things they love to do—and need to do—day to day. For children and adults with ADHD, anxiety, autism, and many neurological disorders, equine or horse therapy has proven to dramatically lower overall levels of anxiety. The basis of the therapy is the connection that patients can make with their horses. This connection is said to be easy because horses behave similarly to humans in their social and responsive behavior. The hour-long sessions were conducted in an indoor arena and included grooming, feeding, and riding. Investigators doing research on this therapy have used MRI brain scans to demonstrate how brain activity, specifically in areas of the brain associated with stress, is turned on during equine therapy.

Art and the Brain

Looking for another way to stimulate some brain growth? If you've got a mind or a passion for music, then you're already on that journey.

Don't Just Sit and Listen…

Studies have shown that there's a connection between musical training and stronger thinking ability, vocabulary, and even how speech is heard and processed. But it's not quite as simple as taking a crash course in electric guitar, regardless of how well you can rock out. In a 2014 study from Northwestern University, to get the most out of a music class, students needed to be fully participating in the class. Researchers studied the brains of students who took a music appreciation class and others who took actual music lessons over the course of two years. Those students who were more actively engaged in the program showed stronger brain understanding of speech and increases in their reading scores—while the less-engaged students didn't show improvements.

Picking up an instrument and learning to play is an ideal way to promote new brain connections.

It makes sense that musicians may have increased brain density in some areas. Professional musicians have to use their ears (to hear the sounds), their eyes (to read the music off the paper), and their limbs (to manipulate their instrument) to make their music. One neuroimaging study showed that string musicians who started performing before 7 years of age had a larger **corpus callosum** than those who started training later. This is the part of the brain that connects the two **hemispheres** together.

Have you ever been sitting listening to somebody lecture at you, say the midst of a class? Does your pencil start to find edges of the pages and begin to make random lines or notes, even words or pictures? We've been drawing and doodling long before we were using verbal language, and the very act of doing so may be a way for your brain to stay active and engaged.

Experimental Doodlers

In a 2009 study, participants listened to a boring phone message for 2 ½ minutes. One group was given paper to doodle with, the other nothing. Interestingly, the group that doodled recalled 29% more information than the group that did not. Meanwhile, a follow-up study focused on doodling in science lessons, which tend to use a lot of visuals such as graphs and charts. Sure enough, the students who doodled were able to retain more information, and had more fun learning, as well.

Some researchers wonder if doodling keeps the brain active by stimulating parts of the brain that keep the cerebral cortex occupied at its baseline activity when concentrating. Doodles may also provide a brain break in the midst of a period of intense concentration. But be warned: in a 2012 study, when doodlers tried to look at and recall a group of images, they had trouble doing so. It may be that their **visual processing** powers were focusing on too many tasks at once—the doodling and the images they were trying to remember.

Brain Stimulation

Reading these very words means you've put your brain to the test. Good readers are activating parts of the brain that are designed to recognize text as letters, words, and phrases in just a fraction of a second. Clusters of neurons in your visual cortex are helping to recognize the patterns in these letters, helping you make meaning of what's on the page. But what's happening beyond the pages of the book? Is someone moving across the room beyond you? And what about those sounds you hear in the background? Are you even paying attention?

Getting Fidgety

Fidget spinners and fidget toys. They might be the rage in your school, or maybe the fad has passed. But we are a species that fidgets and uses our hands to fiddle. Why the need? Could it come from a history of using our hands, whether to make weapons for hunting, and building, or even writing with pencils and paper over the years? Fidgeting might help keep us from getting bored when having to focus our attention in a sustained way, such as when sitting and listening to a teacher at school. A fidget toy might help offset some of your boredom or distraction, but at a certain point, that fidget toy might become a distraction itself.

Top Down, Bottom Up

What does it mean when we talk about paying attention? The good news is that as humans, we have selective attention. This means that we can choose what we want to pay attention to at a given time. This is helpful, given that all of the stimuli around us can be overwhelming. For example, imagine driving into a new city for the first time—you have to pay attention to the road, but there are so many sights there to distract you.

One way scientists classify the way we pay attention is to think of it as Top Down, and Bottom Up. Top-Down processing is attention that you voluntarily spend, for example, on reading, watching TV, or listening to music. You're focusing your attention onto one specific task, such as reading these words right now. Bottom-Up processing is a bit different. It is a stimulus-driven, involuntary means of focusing your attention—such as when you notice things changing in your environment around you, like the headlights of cars getting closer, fireworks going off, or the changing colors of streetlights telling a driver to stop or go.

Training Your Brain in the Internet Age

Once upon a time, people got their information from the printed word. That means books. Like the one you're reading. You might flip through some books, but reading at a measured, or controlled, pace gives you time to think deeply about what you're reading. Books often require readers to read at this pace. Then came the Internet: an ever-growing repository of knowledge, text, videos, and social communication at our fingertips! It's easy to jump from bit to bit of information as we scroll down our screens. But as we are shifting some of our reading from paper to tablets, phones, and screens, what are we gaining? What are we losing? And how is it affecting our brains?

THINK ABOUT IT!

What strategies can you think of that would help you focus, despite the digital distractions you deal with every day? Could the Internet help you create new connections in your brain, too? How?

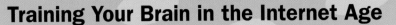

This is Your Brain on the Internet

Some scientists suggest that the way we engage with the Internet is changing the wiring of our brains. The quick "power browsing" in which we scan through information is a key skill when there's so much content out there—think about trying to sift through a Google search for information about rhinoceroses, for example. As you go through all of that information, the synapses associated with short-term memory are getting stronger, but what's happening to our ability to focus and concentrate more deeply?

Researchers have been exploring these questions with the rise of access to the Internet. A 2009 study at Stanford University explored differences in the ways light and heavy media "multitaskers" could process information. In the study, the heavier media multitaskers didn't do as well as light multitaskers when performing a test in which they had to switch tasks. Researchers noticed that the subjects had trouble separating pieces of information in their minds. This suggests that heavy media multitaskers have a harder time deciding which information is helpful, and which information is irrelevant.

Mind Your Memory

If brain plasticity involves making deep connections to create new neural pathways, then what happens when things get in the way of making those deep connections? In a 2016 study, researchers from the University of California and the University of Illinois explored how likely we are to rely on our memory or use the Internet to find information. Participants were put into groups to find the answers to some trivia questions—either using their memory, or using an Internet search. Both groups could answer the easy questions by using memory or the Internet. But the participants who had already used the Internet to find the answers were more likely to keep using the Internet rather than those who had used their memory. They did this even for the simple questions that they could have answered without an Internet search. The researchers suggest that our memory is changing, and that we are tending to use the Internet to help us remember facts rather than processing them in our brains.

WRAP IT UP!

In this book, you've learned that your brain never stops learning. If you employ a growth mindset and use strategies, help from others, and new experiences to help create new connections in your brain, you can actually increase the volume of some parts of your brain and change its structure. Scientists and researchers still have much to learn about the brain. Imagine the possibilities! This diagram should give your brain a refresher on all of the parts we mentioned in this book.

PREFRONTAL CORTEX

Part of the cerebrum, this part of the brain allows you to make decisions, think critically, and learn complex new things.

cell body

Your brain and nervous system are made up of neurons and other cells. Neurons connect to one another through axons, synapses, and dendrites. Your brain can add and reorganize the connections between neurons as you strengthen different skills or learn new things.

dendrites

axon

myelin

PARIETAL LOBE

Also part of the cerebrum, the parietal lobes control your movement and your spatial awareness, or how aware you are of your own body in relation to the space and objects around it.

CEREBRUM

Making up about 75% of your brain's volume, this structure includes the outer layer of the brain, called the cerebral cortex, and some inner parts of the brain such as the hippocampus. The cerebral cortex includes parts of the brain such as the prefrontal cortex and the brain's many lobes.

Insula—Located deep in the cerebral cortex, the insula deals with sensory perception and complex emotional responses, such as empathy.

Hippocampus – Located in the temporal lobe, the hippocampus is part of the limbic system, and stores your long-term and short-term memories.

Amygdala – Located in the limbic system deep within the brain, the amygdala controls your emotional reactions to stimuli and events.

BIBLIOGRAPHY

BOOKS

Boaler, Jo. *Mathematical Mindsets*. Jossey-Bass, 2016.

Carr, Nicholas. *The Shallows: What The Internet Is Doing To Our Brains*. W.W. Norton & Company, 2010.

Costandi, Moheb. *Neuroplasticity*. The MIT Press, 2016.

Fotuhi, Majid, M.D., Ph.D., *Boost Your Brain*. HarperCollins, 2013.

Funston, Sylvia, and Jay Ingram. *It's All In Your Head: A Guide to Your Brilliant Brain*. Maple Tree Press, 2005

Simpson, Kathleen. *The Human Brain: Inside Your Body's Control Room*. National Geographic, 2009.

Sweeney, Michael S. *Brainworks: The Mind-Bending Science of How You See, What You Think, and Who You Are*. National Geographic, 2011.

ARTICLES

Williams, Florence. This Is Your Brain On Nature. *National Geographic*, (January 2016): 54–67

ACADEMIC STUDIES

Maguire, E.A., D.G. Gadian, I.S. Johnsrude, C.D. Good, J. Ashburner, R.S. Frackowiak, and C.D. Frith. "Navigation-related structural change in the hippocampi of taxi drivers." Proceedings of the National Academy of Sciences, 97(8) (2000): 4398–4403.

Mechelli, A., J.T. Crinion, U. Noppeney, J. O'Doherty, J. Ashburner, R.S. Frackowiak, and C.J. Price. "Structural plasticity in the bilingual brain." *Nature* 431(7010)(2004): 757.

Woollett, K., and E.A. Maguire. "Acquiring 'the Knowledge' of London's Layout Drives Structural Brain Changes." *Current Biology* 21(24)(2011):2109–2114.

WEBSITES

www.theglobeandmail.com/arts/books-and-media/the-woman-who-changed-her-brain-barbara-arrowsmith-young/article4225057/

www.theatlantic.com/education/archive/2016/12/how-praise-became-a-consolation-prize/510845/

https://web.stanford.edu/~paunesku/articles/claro_2016.pdf

news.psu.edu/story/334349/2014/11/12/ research/learning-languages-workout-brains-both-young-and-old

time.com/3634995/study-kids-engaged-music-class-for-benefits-northwestern/

www.wsj.com/articles/the-power-of-the-doodle-improve-your-focus-and-memory-1406675744

www.pnas.org/content/106/37/15583. abstract?sid=113b39d8-d0b5-4f46-b2a5-362ee79d0b61

www.tandfonline.com/doi/full/10.1080/096 58211.2016.1210171

LEARNING MORE

BOOKS

Fremder, Gloria. *Learning to Learn: Strengthening Study Skills and Brain Power.* Incentive Publications, 2013.

Swanson, Jennifer. *Brain Games: The Mind-Blowing Science of Your Amazing Brain.* National Geographic Kids, 2015.

Woodward, John. *How to be a Genius.* Dorling Kindersley, 2013.

WEBSITES

Visit this website to access free, weekly tool tips and other information to learn additional strategies and brain-centered research.
www.brainsmart.org/-Free-Strategies

This website offers helpful information and strategies about how best to study.
https://ww2.kqed.org/mindshift/2014/08/25/how-does-the-brain-learn-best-smart-studying-strategies/

Frontiers for Young Minds offers many interesting articles about the brain and neuroplasticity—edited by kids!
https://kids.frontiersin.org/article/10.3389/frym.2014.00005

GLOSSARY

adrenaline A hormone given off in the body during times of stress. Adrenaline increases breathing rates and blood circulation rates, and prepares the muscles in the body to flee.

amygdala The part of the brain that controls emotions

anterior insula region A part of the brain that deals with emotional responses, such as empathy

anxiety A disorder that involves extreme feelings of worry or nervousness, and sometimes causes panic attacks

axons The long, threadlike parts of neurons that send messages to other neurons

blind spot An area on the retina of the eye where a person's view is obstructed

blood pressure The force of blood on the walls of blood vessels, such as veins and arteries

cardiovascular Relating to the heart and blood vessels

cell body The part of the cell that contains its nucleus, which is similar to the brain of a cell

corpus callosum The part of the brain that joins the right and left hemispheres of the brain

cortex The outer layer of the brain, made up of gray matter

dendrites The short, branch-like parts of a cell that receives messages from other cells and transmits the messages to the cell body

depression A disorder that involves extreme feelings of sadness and hopelessness, often coupled with a lack of energy, sleep, and appetite

diagnosed Identified as having a medical condition

executive functions Processes and skills, controlled by the prefrontal cortex in the brain, that have to do with managing onself, such as goal-setting, planning, multitasking, focusing, and controlling impulses

fixed mindset A term coined by Carol Dweck that describes the belief that one's skills and knowledge are set, or unchanging

gray matter Darker tissue of the brain that contains cell bodies of neurons and their dendrites

growth mindset A term coined by Carol Dweck that describes the belief that one's skills and knowledge can be trained and developed through hard work and help from others

hemispheres The two halves of a sphere, such as the brain

hippocampus The part of the brain that has to do with memory

hormones Substances in the body that make certain cells or parts of the body work in certain ways

insulin A hormone that regulates the amount of sugar in the blood

left inferior parietal lobe The part of the brain that is involved in perceiving facial emotions and that processes different kinds of stimuli at the same time

matter Anything that takes up space and has mass

meditation Thinking deeply or focusing on something

neurogenesis The growth of cells in the nervous system

optic nerve The nerve that transmits signals from the eye to the brain

parasympathetic nervous system The part of the autonomic, or involuntary, nervous system that works to relax the body by slowing down some functions, such as heart rate

recalibrate Reassess or re-adjust

relaxation response A stress-management technique that induces relaxation in the body

self-regulating Controlling one's own actions

states of meditation The condition of the body during different types of meditation

sympathetic nervous system The part of the autonomic, or involuntary, nervous system that creates a fight-or-flight response by speeding up some body functions, such as breathing rate

visual-spatial information Information and skills that help us understand the relationships between objects that we can see

visual processing The process of taking in visual information through our eyes and understanding that information in the brain

INDEX

About the Authors
Jeff Szpirglas and Danielle Saint-Onge work as authors and teachers. Jeff has written numerous books for young readers focusing on themes such as fear, and unusual human behavior. He is also passionate about horror stories. When taking a break from being the school librarian and writing books, Danielle runs her own private coaching practice. She works one-on-one with children and families experiencing executive functioning difficulties. Both Jeff and Danielle are passionate educators who believe in writing books that reflect the experiences and lives of the students they teach.